I'm lonely

WAYLAND

Your Feelings

I'm bored
I'm lonely
I'm worried
It's not fair

First published in 1997 by
Wayland Publishers Ltd
61 Western Road, Hove
East Sussex BN3 1JD, England

© Copyright 1997 Wayland Publishers Limited

Series editor: Alex Woolf
Designer: Jean Wheeler

British Library Cataloguing in Publication Data

Moses, Brian, 1950 -
    I'm lonely. - (Your feelings)
      1.Loneliness - Juvenile literature
      I.Title II.Gordon, Mike, 1948 -
      155.9'2

Hardback ISBN 0-7502-2038-4

Paperback ISBN 0-7502-2130-5

Typeset by Jean Wheeler
Printed and bound in Italy by G. Canale & C.S.p.A., Turin

I'm lonely

Written by Brian Moses

Illustrated by Mike Gordon

WAYLAND

When I'm lonely I feel like...

a single cactus
in a desert...

a kite that's
been left in
a tree...

4

the last puppy
in the pet shop
window.

When I'm lonely...

I pretend that
I don't care.

6

I try hard not to
be miserable.

I play with my pets.

8

I talk to
Grandma on
the telephone.

When everyone
has gone on holiday
except for me,
I feel lonely.

But when they
send me postcards
it helps to know
    that they're
thinking of me.

When mum's time is taken up with my baby sister...

I feel lonely.

But then my sister
wants *me* to bath her
and I feel wanted again.

When I'm left in the classroom to finish my work while everyone else is outside...

I feel lonely.

But I finish it really quickly
and race out to join them.

But I know Mum and Dad are only a phone call away.

18

When I feel lonely it helps if I listen to a tape or watch a favourite programme on television.

It helps if I read my
books and imagine
I'm somewhere else...

or try to make friends with
somebody new.

Sometimes grownups can be lonely too. My Gran says she felt lonely when Grandad had to go into hospital. For how long?

My Dad says he felt lonely when Mum and I went to visit Mum's sister for a week.

Mum says my sister feels lonely when I go to school and she's left to play on her own.

She's always pleased to see me when I come home.

Sometimes you can even feel lonely when there are lots of other people around...

when no one wants to play with you in the playground...

on your first day
at a new school...

at a party where you don't know anyone.

Perhaps you know someone
who might be feeling lonely?

What could you
do to help?

Notes for parents and teachers

Read the book with children either individually or in groups. Question them about how they feel when they are lonely. Which of the ideas on pages 4–5 is the closest to how they feel? Or do they picture their loneliness in different ways? Ask them to illustrate how they feel.

Ask children to suggest some images for loneliness:
Being lonely is having no one to wish you a happy birthday.
Being lonely is an old man sitting on a park bench on Christmas Day.
Being lonely is a rabbit peering through the wire of a tiny hutch.

Much of the book looks at situations in which children often feel lonely. Talk about the positive measures that can be taken to make children feel less lonely. How should you treat a new girl or boy in your school? What can children do to help themselves? Children might like to act out a scene where a new child is reassured about how good life will be at the new school.

Listen to the Ralph McTell song 'Streets of London'. Talk about the lyrics and encourage children to talk about occasions when they have seen homeless people. How can we help people who are in this situation? Whilst we might think we are lonely from time to time, are we ever really lonely when we compare ourselves to some of the characters in this song?

Collect other words that we use to describe being lonely: 'friendless', 'deserted', 'forsaken', 'lonesome'. Is being alone the same thing as being lonely?

Can children think of people who choose to be alone for one reason or another?

Books to read

Little Beaver and the Echo written by Amy Macdonald, illustrated by Sarah Fox-Davies (Walker Books, 1990). Little Beaver is lonely living on his own at the edge of a pond. One day he starts to cry and hears someone else crying on the other side of the pond. So Little Beaver sets off to find a friend.

Gorilla by Anthony Browne (Walker Books, 1983). This is a lovely tale of a lonely girl, a friendly gorilla and the fun and adventures they share.

The Spring Rabbit by Joyce Dunbar and Susan Varley (Collins Picture Lions, 1995). Smudge, a little rabbit, feels lonely. He has no brothers and sisters to play with. Then everything changes when Spring arrives.

Little Bean by John Wallace (Collins, 1996). Little Bean's Daddy is always too busy to play or read to her. She misses her Daddy and then one day he discovers that he misses his daughter too.

Gus and Nipper by Rodney Peppe (Collins, 1996). Gus is a cat who leans too far out of a train window and falls out. He feels very lonely on his own until he meets up with a mouse called Nipper and a strange friendship begins.